SCIENCE MAKERS

Making with
STATES OF MATTER

Anna Claybourne

BUILD AMAZING PROJECTS WITH INSPIRATIONAL SCIENTISTS, ARTISTS AND ENGINEERS

First published in Great Britain in 2018 by Wayland
Copyright © Hodder and Stoughton, 2018

Editor: Sarah Silver
Designer: Eoin Norton
Picture researcher: Diana Morris

ISBN 978 1 5263 0548 0

MIX
Paper from responsible sources
FSC® C104740
FSC www.fsc.org

Printed in China

Wayland, an imprint of
Hachette Children's Group
Part of Hodder and Stoughton
Carmelite House
50 Victoria Embankment
London EC4Y 0DZ

An Hachette UK Company
www.hachette.co.uk
www.hachettechildrens.co.uk

CONTENTS

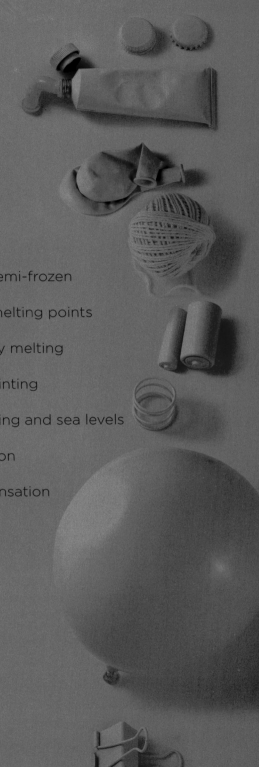

4   **Making changes**

6   **Chocolate art** | Science: melting and freezing

8   **Summer slushies** | Science: freezing and melting, semi-frozen

10   **Crayon creations** | Science: melting and freezing, melting points

12   **Instant ice cream** | Science: freezing and cooling by melting

14   **Glue gun art** | Science: melting and freezing, 3D printing

16   **Melting ice people** | Science: melting, global warming and sea levels

18   **Desert cooler** | Science: cooling through evaporation

20   **Save your life at sea** | Science: evaporation, condensation

24   **Evaporation art** | Science: evaporation, crystals

26   **Recycled paper** | Science: evaporation, fibres

30   **Glossary and further information**

32   **Index**

TAKE CARE!

These projects can be made with everyday objects, materials and tools that you can find at home, or in a supermarket, hobby store or DIY store. However, some do involve working with things that are sharp or breakable, or need extra strength to operate. Make sure you have an adult on hand to supervise and to help with anything that could be dangerous, and get permission before you try out any of the projects.

MAKING CHANGES

Water vapour floating in the air

Liquid water

Solid water (ice)

Our world, and all the real, 3D stuff around us, is made of matter. Water, air, metal, rock, chocolate, a book, a glass window, a plastic bottle – all these things are made of different types of matter.

Matter can change between three main 'states of matter' – solid, liquid and gas. For example, we usually think of water as a liquid, but it can also be solid, frozen ice, or invisible water vapour, a gas.

CHANGES OF STATE

When matter changes between a solid and a liquid, or a liquid and a gas, it's called a change of state. Changes of state happen a lot in everyday life. For example:

- **Chocolate melts in your mouth, or when you cook with it**

- **Wet washing dries when the water evaporates into the air**

- **We freeze water to make ice cubes**

- **The lava from a volcano is melted rock. It hardens again to make new, solid rock**

- **Water vapour from the air condenses into droplets on a cold surface**

Water vapour floating in the air

Solid ice

Liquid water

Cold glass

Water vapour in air condenses into drops

HOW IT WORKS

Changes of state happen because of changes of temperature. It's all to do with the tiny atoms and molecules that matter is made of, and how temperature affects them.

 In a solid, the molecules are tightly packed and don't move much.

 In a liquid, the particles can flow and move past each other.

 In a gas, the particles are far apart and zoom around.

HEAT AND MATTER

As matter **heats up,** the molecules gain more energy, and move more.

As matter **cools down,** the molecules lose energy, and move less.

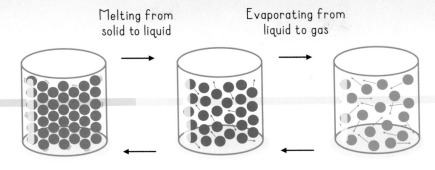

Melting from solid to liquid

Evaporating from liquid to gas

Freezing from liquid to solid

Condensing from gas to liquid

Chocolate is melted so it can be poured into moulds to make different shapes.

USING THE CHANGES

Changes of state are used in all kinds of everyday activities and inventions. For example, steam power is one of the most important inventions ever. It works by boiling water to make steam (hot water vapour – a gas). This creates a pushing force to power machines, or to turn turbines to generate electricity. A fridge works by evaporating a chemical to remove heat. Many foods are made by evaporating, freezing or melting, such as dried fruit, concentrated drinks, ice cream, powdered milk and chocolate.

CHANGES IN ART

Artists have always relied on changes of state to make their work. Clay and paint have to dry though evaporation, and melted wax is used to make casts for statues. Increasingly, artists are also using changes of state in their artwork, such as a sculpture that changes over time, by evaporating or melting.

A temporary sculpture, made of ice and left to melt in the sun.

CHOCOLATE ART

Make a portrait or picture entirely from chocolate – perfect as a birthday card!

MAKER PROFILE:

Prudence Staite
(1979–)

Prudence Staite is a food artist who combines art and cooking skills to make paintings, sculptures and everyday objects out of food. She's known for her chocolate artworks and other creations, including chocolate portraits and statues, a chocolate maze, a chocolate cake motorbike and a chocolate sofa.

Prudence Staite's chocolate version of the famous painting *The Scream*, by Edvard Munch.

WHAT YOU NEED

- three 100 g bars of chocolate: one dark, one milk and one white
- small foil cooking tray
- tea towel
- small saucepan
- knife
- chopping board
- three bowls that fit over the saucepan
- three spoons
- three small sealable sandwich bags
- scissors
- aluminium foil
- cake decorations
- plate

I could not decide whether to become a chef or an artist. I wanted to be both.
– *Prudence Staite*

Step 1.

If your foil tray's base isn't flat, rub it with a tea towel to smooth it out. Unwrap one bar of chocolate and (with an adult to help) chop it into small pieces. Put half of it into a bowl.

6

Step 2.
Ask an adult to heat some water in the saucepan until almost boiling. Take it off the heat, and rest the bowl of chocolate over the pan. Stir until the chocolate is nearly melted.

Step 3.
Remove the bowl and stir in the rest of the chopped chocolate, which will also melt. Repeat this for the other two bars, so you have three bowls of melted chocolate.

Step 4.
Spoon each type of chocolate into separate sandwich bags, and seal them closed. With scissors, snip a tiny corner of each bag. They can now be squeezed to draw chocolate lines.

Step 5.
Practise first on a piece of foil if you like. Then you can start drawing on the base of the foil tray. Build up your pictures using different chocolate colours. Use some cake decorations to add colour and sparkle.

Step 6.
When your picture is finished, add more chocolate to make a layer about 1 cm deep, and smooth the surface gently with a spoon. Leave to set in a cool place for several hours.

Step 7.
Turn the tray upside down over a plate, and gently press the picture out. Use a tea towel to do the pressing so that your hands don't melt the chocolate.

MELT AND FREEZE

Though your chocolate never gets icy cold, when you make chocolate art, you are melting and freezing. As a melted liquid, you can use the chocolate to draw and paint. Then you let it set, or freeze again, so that it's solid. The melting and freezing point of water is 0°C (-32°F) which feels very cold. But for chocolate, it's around 32°C (90°F).

TOP TIP

Remember that the parts you do first will come out 'on top' when you turn the pictures out.

To give your picture as a present, put it in a food gift bag and tie with a ribbon. It will melt easily, so keep it cool and give it the same day if you can.

SUMMER SLUSHIES

Omar Knedlik invented refreshing, half-frozen slushy drinks by accident, then built a machine to make them. They're easy to make at home too.

MAKER PROFILE:

Omar Knedlik
(1916–1989)

In the 1950s, Omar Knedlik owned an ice cream cafe in Kansas, USA, where it gets very hot in summer. His soda fountain, which dispensed cold drinks, stopped working, so he put bottles of soda in the freezer to cool down. If he left them too long, he found that they turned into a semi-frozen slush – which his customers loved! The drinks were so popular, Knedlik adapted an old ice-cream machine to make more slush. Working with an air-conditioner company, he developed this into a purpose-built machine, called the ICEE machine.

Slush drinks are now popular around the world.

WHAT YOU NEED

- concentrated squash or cordial
- water
- two cups of ice cubes
- measuring cup (or any average-sized cup)
- food processor or hand-held blender
- jug or large bowl
- large spoon
- drinking straws
- glass for serving
- food colouring (optional)

1.

Step 1.
Make up one glass of squash or cordial with water, making it about three times stronger than you normally would (as it's going to be mixed with the ice as well).

2.

Step 2.
Ask an adult to get the blender ready. Measure out two cups of ice cubes, and put them into the food processor or jug or large bowl. Pour in the glass of squash or cordial as well.

3.

Step 3.
Ask the adult to switch the food processor or hand blender on, and blend the mixture in short pulses. Keep blending until it turns into a thick, lumpy slush.

4.

Step 4.
Spoon the slush into glasses and add straws and fruit decorations if you like. Drink as soon as possible, before it melts!

COOL COLOURS

If you use squash or cordial with a strong colour, such as blackcurrant, you'll get a brightly coloured slushy. If you're using a paler flavour, such as lemon, you can add a few drops of food colouring to brighten it up.

ICE SOUP

A slushy drink is halfway between a frozen ice lolly and a normal drink. Instead of being a solid lump of ice, it has lots of small chunks of ice, with some liquid in between – a bit like a thick soup. This means you can drink the slushy easily, or slurp it up through a straw.

You can't keep the slushy in the freezer, as it would soon become rock-hard. Instead, slushy machines keep the mixture just below freezing, and keep it moving, so that the lumps of ice can't freeze together.

CRAYON CREATIONS

Make multicoloured wax crayons using the power of melting and freezing.

MAKER PROFILE:

Edwin Binney
(1866–1934)

In the late 1800s, Edwin Binney and his cousin Harold Smith owned a company that made pigments, or colour chemicals. One of their products was a type of pencil for children to use at school. When Binney and Smith asked teachers what other things they needed, they asked for cheap, colourful crayons. Artists' pastels made with oil or wax did already exist, but they were expensive, and toxic. So Edwin Binney developed the first children's crayons, made from hard wax mixed with safe pigments, formed into pointed sticks. His wife, Alice Stead Binney, came up with a name for them – 'Crayola'.

WHAT YOU NEED

- wax crayons in lots of different colours
- a non-stick muffin baking tray
- an oven
- oven gloves
- paper

1.

Step 1.
Peel all the paper wrappers off the crayons, if they have them. Break the crayons into smaller pieces and put different combinations of colours into the spaces in the tray.

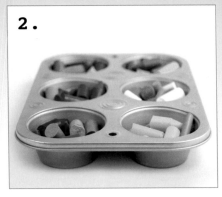

Step 2.

Make sure the crayons don't stick up above the edges of the muffin cups, or else the wax will overflow when the crayons melt.

Step 3.

Ask an adult to heat the oven to about 80°C. Then they should put the muffin tray in the oven for about 10 minutes.

Step 4.

If the crayons have melted, ask an adult to remove the tray and leave it to cool. If they haven't quite melted, leave them for another 5 or 10 minutes.

Step 5.

Once the tray and the wax are completely cold, you can pop the new crayons out. Turn the tray over and tap on the back of it to release them.

MULTICOLOUR MIXTURES:

Put similar colours together to make a themed crayon – such as greens and browns for a forest crayon, or pink, orange and yellow for a sunset crayon. Or mix all the colours for a rainbow crayon. Use the edge of the crayon for a multicoloured effect.

A blow moulding machine making plastic bottles.

MELT IT, MOULD IT

Crayons are made by mixing pigments with melted wax. The liquid mixture is poured into moulds, where it freezes, or sets hard, in the shape of the moulds. The same thing happens when you melt the crayons again to make multicoloured crayons.

In fact, thousands of everyday objects – crayons, buttons, toys, bottles, phone cases, kitchen tools, even parts of cars and planes – are made by melting a material (such as metal or plastic), pouring it into a mould to shape it, and letting it set solid again.

INSTANT
ICE CREAM

Make your own ice cream the way they did before freezers – using ice, salt and motion.

MAKER PROFILE:

Nancy Johnson
(1795–1890)

Not much is known about the life of Nancy Johnson. But we do know that in 1843, she patented a brilliant invention that made it much easier to make ice cream. Previously, people made ice cream in a container surrounded with ice and salt, scraping the mixture off the sides as it froze. It was hard work and took hours. Johnson's device had a handle that moved a paddle around inside the machine, constantly moving the mixture inwards from the sides, while the lid kept it cold. Home ice-cream makers still work in a similar way today.

WHAT YOU NEED

- two sealable plastic food bags, one small, one large
- enough ice cubes to fill the large bag
- half a cup of salt
- 1 cup of full-fat milk
- half a teaspoon of vanilla essence or flavouring
- two level tablespoons of sugar
- mixing bowl or jug
- towel or tea towel
- serving bowl, spoon and sprinkles

A later version of Johnson's invention

1.

Step 1.

Measure the milk, vanilla and sugar into the bowl or jug, and stir well. Pour the mixture into the small food bag. Squeeze out as much air as possible, then seal the bag tightly.

2.

3.

Step 2.
Fill the large food bag with ice cubes, and pour in the salt. Close the bag and shake the ice cubes around to cover them in salt.

Step 3.
Open the bag of ice, and carefully push the smaller bag of milk into the middle, so that it's surrounded by salty ice cubes. Seal the ice cube bag up again.

4.

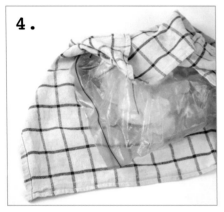

5.

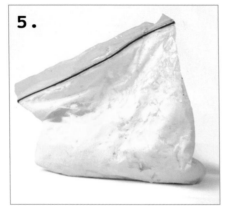

6.

Step 4.
Shake and squeeze the ice cube bag for several minutes. It will get very cold, so wrap it in a towel to keep your hands from freezing.

Step 5.
After about 5 minutes of squeezing and shaking, feel the milk inside the smaller bag – it should have turned to ice cream! If not, shake it for a couple more minutes.

Step 6.
When the ice cream is ready, take the small bag out, and quickly rinse it under a cold tap to get any salt off. Scoop the ice cream into a bowl, and eat immediately!

Try making different flavours of ice cream using strawberry or chocolate milk. Milk alternatives work too, such as soya or oat milk.

SALT SCIENCE

Why do you add salt to the ice? Although ice on its own would make the milk cold, adding salt makes it colder. Salt lowers the freezing point of water. This means it's harder for the ice to stay frozen, and it starts to melt. But melting uses heat, so the ice takes heat from its surroundings — including the milk mixture, which freezes quickly. The shaking helps all of the milk to touch the cold ice and turn to ice cream.

GLUE GUN ART

Use a hot glue gun like a freehand 3D printer,
to create strings, shapes and sculptures.

MAKER PROFILE:

Yasuaki Onishi
(1979–)

Japanese artist Yasuaki Onishi is a pioneer in the use of hot glue in modern art. In his sculptures, strings of white glue, sometimes dotted with crystals, drape down from ropes or tree branches, connecting them to the ground.

The sculptures can fill a room in a gallery, creating a mysterious landscape. Onishi has described how the glue acts as a trace, showing the path of the artist's movements, and revealing the effects of gravity.

Yasuaki Onishi's 2013 work *Vertical Emptiness FP*, made with tree branches and hot glue.

WHAT YOU NEED

- old newspapers
- hot glue gun
- spare glue sticks
- silicon baking sheet or paper, baking parchment paper, or aluminium foil
- baby oil or petroleum jelly
- kitchen roll
- glitter, beads or string (optional)

1.

Step 1.
Choose a workspace close to an electric socket for the glue gun. Spread out some old newspapers to protect the area. On top, spread out your silicon sheet, parchment or foil.

Use kitchen roll to clean the glue gun nozzle when you need to.

2.

3.

4&5.

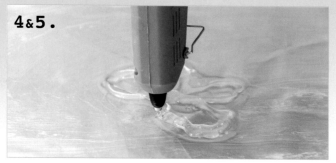

Step 2 .
Rub the silicon sheet, parchment or foil with baby oil or petroleum jelly, so that the glue won't stick to it permanently. Wash your hands afterwards.

Step 3.
Ask an adult to plug in the glue gun to heat up, and supervise while you use it. Take care not to touch the hot nozzle of the gun, or the hot glue as it comes out.

Step 4.
Once the gun is hot, you can start squirting the glue out on to the sheet to make patterns, shapes and even 3D objects. See below for some ideas!

Step 5.
Let the glue cool and set for about 10 minutes before carefully peeling your glue art objects off the backing.

GLUE ART IDEAS

Snowflake
Sprinkle with white glitter.

Flowers
Add beads and glitter to decorate.

Spider web
Connect the crossing lines with smaller lines starting from the centre. Add hanging loops to attach to a window.

PRINTING BY HAND

Some types of printing, including 3D printing, work in a similar way to a glue gun. A nozzle moves around and hot liquid ink or melted plastic come out to form patterns or build up shapes once the liquid hardens. When glue guns became widely used, artists and crafters soon realised they could use them to create objects, as well as for sticking things together. The clear, frosty-looking glue is especially good for modelling water and ice.

Waterfall
Make a waterfall by draping glue over foil folded over a box or jar. When dry, position the waterfall on some stones.

Necklace letters
Make letters and add loops to hang them up.

15

MELTING ICE PEOPLE

Make little model people out of ice, using a modelling clay mould. Then let them melt ... or live in your freezer!

MAKER PROFILE:

Néle Azevedo
(1950–)

Néle Azevedo is a Brazilian sculptor. She's famous for her public artworks made up of hundreds of small human figures moulded from ice. They sit outside in city squares or markets, and gradually melt and drip away in the sun. Azevedo began making the ice people as an alternative 'monument'. Unlike a long-lasting metal or stone statue, they represent ordinary, unknown people, and the fragility of life. However, her work has also been used to symbolise the danger and speed of global warming.

Azevedo's ice people melt in the sun in Berlin, Germany, in 2009.

WHAT YOU NEED

- large block of modelling clay
- rolling pin
- rectangular plastic food container
- baby oil or vaseline (petroleum jelly)
- metal cutlery
- jug of water
- a freezer

The melting ice well depicts this urgency we are living in.
– *Néle Azevedo*

1.

Step 1.
Roll out the modelling clay into a smooth rectangle shape, about 4-5 cm deep. Put it inside your food container and press it down so that it sticks to the base.

2.

Step 2.
Press a human figure shape into the modelling clay, using your fingers and cutlery. A small spoon makes a good head shape. Use spoon or fork handles to make arms and legs.

3.

Step 3.
Make the arms and legs quite thick, as this will make the figure stronger and easier to remove. Press the shape deep into the modelling clay, without breaking through at the bottom.

4.

Step 4.
Use a butter knife to make broad, flat feet to help your ice person to stand up. When the mould is ready, rub the inside surface with petroleum jelly or baby oil.

5.

Step 5.
Put the container next to the freezer, and fill the mould with water. Carefully put it on a flat surface inside the freezer. (Don't worry if a bit of water spills into the container.)

6.

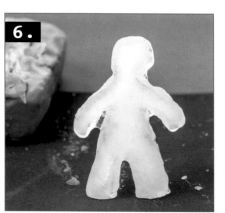

Step 6.
Leave the ice person for 24 hours to freeze solid. Then take it out of the freezer, and let it thaw slightly for about 20 minutes. Then pick up the modelling clay block, and carefully peel the modelling clay away.

MELTING IN THE HEAT

A solid ice block or other shape doesn't melt immediately in warm surroundings. Instead, it will melt from the outside in, dripping and gradually shrinking away. The same thing is happening to some of the world's glaciers and ice caps, as global temperatures increase. Gases such as carbon dioxide, released into the air by burning fuel, are partly causing this, as they help to trap the sun's heat.

STAND ME UP!

Your ice person should be able to stand up, but if not, hold it in a standing position and rub its feet on a flat surface to make them flatter and more stable.

DESERT COOLER

Make a simple fridge that doesn't need electricity, using two flowerpots. Perfect for camping!

MAKER PROFILE:

Mohammed Bah Abba
(1964–2010)

Mohammed Bah Abba came from a family of clay pot makers in Nigeria. He eventually became a teacher, and used his knowledge to develop a simple refrigerator made from two pots. As many people in hot, dry northern Africa don't have an electricity supply, this was incredibly useful, helping to preserve food and reduce disease. Abba hired workers to make thousands of the fridges for local families.

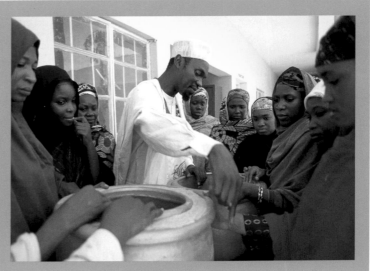

WHAT YOU NEED

- two large unglazed clay or terracotta flowerpots, one bigger than the other (see box)
- strong tape or duct tape
- old newspapers
- about 2 kg of sand (available from garden centres)
- tablespoon
- tea towel
- watering can or jug of water
- sandwich bags
- food to keep cold
- thermometer (optional)

THE RIGHT POTS

Your two pots must be unglazed (they should be rough and matt, not shiny) both inside and outside. They should be the same shape, but different sizes, so that one can fit right inside the other with a bit of space around it.

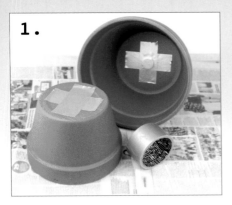

Step 1.
Spread out newspaper on the floor (or make your cooler outdoors). If your pots have drainage holes, tape over the holes firmly.

Step 2.
Put some sand in the bottom of the larger pot, so that you can stand the smaller pot inside with the rims of both pots at the same level.

Step 3.
With your hand along the edge of the smaller pot to keep sand out, start tipping sand down the gap between the two pots, using the tablespoon.

Step 4.
When the gap is full, slowly pour water into the sand, using the jug or watering can. Adding water will make the sand sink down, so fill in the gaps with more sand.

Step 5.
Wrap your food in sandwich bags, and put it inside your cooler. Dampen a tea towel, and lie it on top of the cooler. Leave the cooler somewhere dry and well-ventilated.

Step 6.
Add more water to the sand about twice a day. If you have a weather thermometer or food thermometer, you can test the temperature inside and outside your cooler.

> You should see the pots becoming wet as water soaks into them.

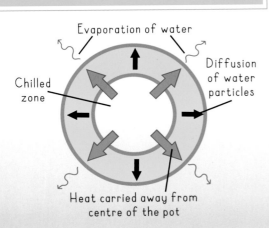

Evaporation of water

Diffusion of water particles

Chilled zone

Heat carried away from centre of the pot

KEEPING COOL

Though Abba developed the idea using two pots, people have known for millennia that damp, unglazed pots keep things cool. It works using evaporation. As water evaporates into the air from the outer pot, it takes heat from the inside, which then cools down – exactly the same way as sweat works on your skin. If the sand is kept wet, the water keeps evaporating, and the fridge stays cool. But it only works well in dry conditions, when the water can evaporate easily.

The cooler will keep working as long as you keep it damp, but won't get as cold as an electric fridge. It's great for keeping drinks cool, but avoid using it for food that goes off quickly, such as meat or fish.

19

MAKER PROFILE:

Maria Telkes
(1900–1995)

Maria Telkes was born in Hungary, but moved to the USA to work as a scientist there. She was fascinated by the power of sunlight, and how solar energy could be used. Among other things, she developed solar heating systems for houses, a solar-powered oven, and early solar panels, gaining herself the nickname 'the sun queen'.

In the early 1940s, during the Second World War (1939–1945), Dr. Telkes worked on a way to provide fresh water for sailors in life rafts, whose ships had been torpedoed and sunk. Her portable solar still used the sun's energy to evaporate salt water, leaving the salt behind. The pure water then condensed and could be collected, making it safe to drink.

SAVE YOUR LIFE AT SEA

Stuck in a life raft, miles from land, with nothing but seawater to drink? This brilliant, easy-to-make invention is the answer.

Sunlight will be used as a source of energy sooner or later ... Why wait?
– Maria Telkes

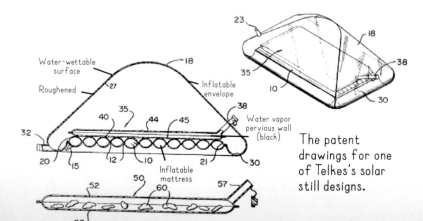

The patent drawings for one of Telkes's solar still designs.

WHAT YOU NEED

- a clear plastic dome, such as a plant cloche
- a clean, dry mixing bowl or salad bowl, the same width as the dome
- a small black plastic plant pot saucer
- strong packing tape or duct tape
- several pieces of clean, black felt
- scissors
- a mixing jug and spoon
- a pack of table salt
- water

PLASTIC DOMES!

There are several types of plastic domes you could use:

You can get a plant cloche at a garden centre

A disposable plastic salad bowl or dessert bowl is another option

1.

Step 1.

If your plant cloche has a plastic hole cover, pull this off. Cover any holes with small pieces of tape, both inside and outside.

2.

Step 2.

Take your bowl and stick a piece of tape across the middle of it, from one side to the other. Put another piece of tape across the bowl at right angles, to make a cross.

3.

Step 3.

Make a small loop of tape, sticky side out, and fix it to the middle of the cross. Gently press the plant pot saucer on to this, so that it is suspended above the middle of bowl.

4.

Step 4.

Cut out four or five circles of black felt that will fit inside the plant pot saucer. Rinse them in cold tap water and wring them out. Stack them in a pile and put them into the saucer.

5.

Step 5.
Half-fill your jug with water from the tap, and stir in about 10 tablespoons of table salt. Taste a tiny bit of the water to make sure it is very salty, like seawater.

6.

Step 6.
Carefully pour salt water on to the felt in the saucer until it is well soaked. Put the plastic dome over the top, so that it sits on the rim of the bowl.

7.

Step 7.
Stand your solar still in a sunny place, such as on a windowsill that is in sunshine for most of the day, or somewhere safe outdoors.

8.

Step 8.
After an hour or two, you should see drops of water collecting on the inside of the dome, and running down into the bowl at the bottom.

9.

Step 9.
Carefully collect some of the water from the bowl with a clean spoon, and see if it tastes fresh. It should not be salty any more, as the salt has been left behind in the black tray.

PURE WATER SCIENCE

Although Maria Telkes invented a still for use on life rafts, she wasn't the first to use this method of removing salt from water. The process, called distillation, was already known about. If you evaporate salty water, the salt will be left behind. The pure water vapour can then condense and turn back into liquid, and the salt-free water can be collected for drinking. It's the same as what happens when the sun evaporates water from the sea, and it falls as fresh, non-salty rain.

Telkes's solar still was especially useful, because it was made to be portable and to work at sea, even in rough weather. The absorbent tray held the salt water in place so it couldn't spill into the pure water. The still could be floated on the surface of the sea, and it was collapsible, so it could be stored away in a small space.

MAKE IT BLACK!

Telkes' still used sunlight to warm the salt water to make it evaporate quickly. The salt water tray is black, because black surfaces are better at absorbing light and heat, while lighter surfaces reflect them.

Modern life rafts today are equipped with solar stills that have a similar design.

WHY CAN'T YOU DRINK SEAWATER?

If you're desperately thirsty, drinking seawater might seem like a good idea – but it isn't! Your body does need some salt in order to work, but you have to drink water as well to dilute it. Seawater contains too much salt. Your kidneys flush the salt out, but there isn't enough water for them to do this properly. So the body becomes dangerously dehydrated, or dried out.

In 1982, American sailor and boat-builder Steve Callahan spent 76 days lost at sea in a life raft, after his boat sank in the Atlantic Ocean. Solar stills were among the emergency supplies he had with him on his raft, and saved his life by giving him a small amount of fresh drinking water each day. Salt stills have saved many other lives too.

EVAPORATION ART

Mix water, salt and ink, leave them to evaporate, and they'll create amazing, changing, unique artworks.

MAKER PROFILE:

Tania Kovats
(1966–)

British artist and sculptor Tania Kovats makes many kinds of art, but is especially fascinated with the world's water – rain, rivers, lakes and seas. In her exhibition *Evaporation*, she made bowls in the shapes of the Earth's oceans, and put coloured salt water in each one. As it evaporated, the mixture left rings and bands of colourful salt crystals. Using evaporation to make art means you can't predict exactly what shapes and patterns will form, and the art changes over time as more liquid evaporates.

WHAT YOU NEED

- a pack of Epsom salts (from a chemist)
- small bowl
- measuring cup
- mixing jug
- tablespoon
- hot tap water
- water-based drawing ink or food colouring in bright colours
- old newspapers
- large bowls
- large sheets of watercolour paper, blotting paper or thick cartridge paper

One of the bowls in Kovat's *Evaporation* exhibition.

The sea is this enormous solvent of everything on the planet.
– *Tania Kovats*

1.

Step 1.
Measure a cup of Epsom salts into the jug, then add a cup of hot tap water. Stir the mixture well until the salts dissolve and disappear.

2.

Step 2.
Pour a little of the mixture into the smaller bowl, and stir in a few drops of ink or food colouring to make the liquid brightly coloured.

3.

4.

Step 3.
Spread out some old newspapers, and put a large bowl in the middle. Put a piece of paper on the bowl, and press on it gently to make it dip down in the middle so the liquid won't run off. Leave it on the bowl while you make the artwork.

Step 4.
Use the tablespoon to drip the coloured liquid on to the paper, and gently spread it around to make a puddle.

5.

Step 5.
Leave the mixture in a safe place to evaporate, away from small children and pets. Check it every hour or so to see how it changes.

GROWING CRYSTALS

Epsom salts is the common name for a type of salt called magnesium sulphate. When it dissolves in water, its molecules separate and mix in with the water. When the water evaporates into the air, the molecules are left behind, and gradually arrange themselves into needle-shaped crystals. Adding ink to the mixture makes brightly coloured crystals.

You can try the same thing with normal table salt, or sodium chloride. The crystals will be a different shape, as table salt is a different chemical with different molecules.

FARMING SALT

Sea salt is collected by letting sea water evaporate in the sun, leaving piles of salt crystals behind.

Workers collect sea salt at a salt farm in Thailand.

RECYCLED PAPER

If you have old waste paper lying around, you can make new paper – just like paper pioneer Matthias Koops.

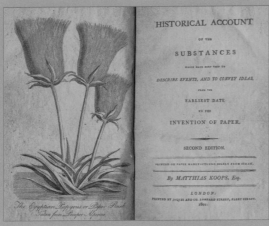

The opening page from a book Koops wrote and printed, using his own straw and wood paper. The book was all about different types of paper!

MAKER PROFILE:

Matthias Koops
(Active around 1800)

Matthias Koops was born in Pomerania, in what is now Germany and Poland, and moved to England in the late 1700s. Though we don't know the dates of his birth and death, we do know that he LOVED paper! At that time, most paper was made from cloth rags, but there was a shortage of them. So Koops tried making paper with straw, thistles, bark and wood. He also came up with a way to recycle old, used paper into new paper, which he called 'regenerated paper'. He then opened a paper factory to make his new products.

WHAT YOU NEED

- waste printer paper, newspaper, drawing paper or envelopes
- large, wide bowl, such as a washing-up bowl
- old newspapers
- scissors
- hot water
- wooden spoon
- two small, plain picture frames about the same size

- mesh
- strong packing tape or duct tape
- rubber gloves
- hand-held electric blender
- large plastic tray or dish
- large pieces of felt or thick cloth
- rolling pin

The art of paper-making ought to be regarded as one of the most useful which has ever been invented.
– Matthias Koops

1.

Step 1.
Spread out old newspapers to work on. Tear or cut up your waste paper into tiny scraps and put them in the bowl. Keep going until you have several large handfuls.

2.

Step 2.
Ask an adult to add hot tap water to the bowl – about twice as much water as the volume of paper. Stir the mixture well and leave it to soak overnight.

3.

Step 3.
Ask an adult to carefully remove the glass and other parts from the picture frames, leaving just the outer frames.

4.

Step 4.
Cut a piece of mesh the same size as one of the frames. Tape it firmly in place all around the edge of the frame. This is called the 'mould'. The other frame should be able to sit neatly on top of the mould. This is called the 'deckle'.

5.

Step 5.
When the paper has soaked, put on the rubber gloves and squeeze and mush it up with your hands. Then ask an adult to blend it to a finer pulp using the handheld blender.

Step 6.
Stir in more water until the paper pulp has a runny texture, like blended soup. Then hold the deckle in place on top of the mould, and submerge them both so that some of the pulp is caught on the mesh as you lift them out.

Step 7.
Move the mould and deckle on to the tray and let the water drain out for a few minutes. Then carefully lift the deckle (top frame) off. The pulp should be left in a rectangle shape.

Step 8.
Put a piece of felt over the rectangle of pulp, and a folded newspaper on top of that. Roll over it firmly with the rolling pin to squeeze more water out of the pulp. Lift off the folded newspaper.

Step 9.
Now carefully turn over the whole mould, with the pulp and felt on it, on to a layer of newspaper. Lift up the mould and gently pull the felt downwards away from the mesh.

Step 10.
The sheet of pulp should come away from the mesh and be left lying on the felt. If it doesn't, use your fingernail to carefully pull the corner of the pulp off the mesh.

Step 11.
Leave the sheet of pulp to dry for at least a day. When it's dry, you'll have a sheet of paper!

FANCY PAPER

• Add dried flower petals to the pulp just after it has settled in the mould.

• Sprinkle the pulp in the mould with glitter.

• Stir water-based ink into the bowl of pulp to colour your paper.

TOO GREY?

If you've used newspaper or printed paper, your recycled paper will look quite grey (although it will become lighter as it dries). If you want paler paper, use waste paper that doesn't have very much ink on it, such as old envelopes.

WATER IN, WATER OUT

Paper is made of lots of tiny little fibres, or string shapes, matted and pressed together. They can come from plants, wood, old cloth or old paper. But to make paper, the fibres have to be mixed with water. This helps the material break down into a mush or pulp, so that the fibres can spread out and form into flat sheets. Then, as the water evaporates away, the fibres stick together and become firm and smooth.

RÉAUMUR AND THE WASPS

Matthias Koops wasn't the first to think of making paper from wood. In 1719, a French scientist, René de Réaumur, noticed how wasps made their papery nests from chewed wood, and suggested we could use it for paper-making too. Koops turned the idea into an industrial process, and today most paper comes from wood.

29

GLOSSARY

atoms Tiny ball-like parts that matter is made from.

carbon dioxide A gas that is produced by some types of living things.

change of state A change from one state of matter to another.

condense To change state from a gas into a liquid.

crystal A mineral that has formed in a regular shape, such as a cube.

dissolve To become broken down into tiny bits in a liquid.

evaporate To change state from a liquid into a gas.

fibre A thread-like or string-like part.

freeze To change state from a liquid into a solid.

freezing point The temperature at which a substance freezes.

gas A state of matter in which molecules are moving fast and are widely spread out.

glacier A slow-moving mass or flow of ice, created by snow falling and collecting.

global warming A gradual increase in the Earth's average temperature.

ice cap A thick layer of ice over a large area, such as a polar region.

liquid A state of matter in which molecules are loosely linked, and can flow and pour.

matter The stuff that all the objects and materials around us are made of.

melt To change state from a solid into a liquid.

melting point The temperature at which a substance melts.

molecules Units of matter made of atoms bonded together.

patent an official right to be the only person allowed to make or sell a new product or invention.

pigment A chemical used to add colour to a substance.

solar To do with the Sun.

solar panel A flat panel made of materials that collect sunlight and convert it into an electric current.

solar power Energy from the sun that is collected and used to generate electricity or power machines.

solid A state of matter in which molecules are tightly packed, and that keeps its shape.

states of matter The forms that matter can exist in, such as solid, liquid or gas.

steam The hot gas that water changes state into when it boils.

still A device used to distil a liquid, by evaporating and then condensing it to remove impurities.

toxic Another word for poisonous.

turbine A wheel-shaped device that rotates when pushed by wind, water, steam or another flowing substance.

water vapour A term used to describe water in the gas state of matter.

FURTHER INFORMATION

WEBSITES

Science Trek: States of Matter Facts
idahoptv.org/sciencetrek/topics/matter/facts.cfm

Exploratorium Science Snacks: States of Matter
www.exploratorium.edu/snacks/
subject/states-of-matter

BBC Bitesize: Solids, Liquids and Gases
www.bbc.co.uk/education/topics/zkgg87h

DK Find Out: What is Matter?
www.dkfindout.com/uk/science/solids-
liquids-and-gases/what-is-matter/

WEBSITES ABOUT MAKING

Tate Kids: Make
www.tate.org.uk/kids/make

PBS Design Squad Global
pbskids.org/designsquad

Instructables
www.instructables.com

Make:
makezine.com

WHERE TO BUY MATERIALS

Hobbycraft
For art and craft materials
www.hobbycraft.co.uk

B&Q
For pipes, tubing, wood, glue and other hardware
www.diy.com

Fred Aldous
For art and craft materials,
photography supplies and books
www.fredaldous.co.uk

BOOKS

Amazing Materials: Solids, liquids and gases
by Rob Colson (Wayland, 2017)

Home Lab by Robert Winston
(Dorling Kindersley, 2016)

Living Things (Science in Infographics)
by Jon Richards (Wayland, 2017)

Mind Webs: Materials by Anna Claybourne
(Wayland, 2014)

Science in a Flash: States of Matter by Georgia
Amson-Bradshaw (Franklin Watts, 2017)

Superpower Science: Masters of Matter
by Joy Lin (Wayland, 2018)

PLACES TO VISIT

The Apsley Paper Trail, Hemel Hempstead, UK
www.thepapertrail.org.uk

Catalyst Science Discovery Centre, Cheshire, UK
www.catalyst.org.uk

The Chocolate Museum, London, UK
www.thechocolatemuseum.co.uk

Science Museum, London, UK
www.sciencemuseum.org.uk

INDEX

Abba, Mohammed Bah 18–19
art/artists 5–6, 14–17, 24
atoms 4
Azevedo, Néle 16

Binney, Edwin 10–11

Callahan, Steve 23
carbon dioxide 17
chocolate 4–7
condensation 4–5, 20–23
coolers, desert 18–19
crayons, wax 10–11
crystals, salt 24–25

distillation 23

electricity 5, 18
energy, solar 20–23
evaporation 4–5, 19–25, 29
Evaporation 24

freezing 4–5, 7–13, 16–17

glaciers 17
global warming 16–17
glue gun 14–15

ice 4–5, 8–9, 12–13, 15–17
ice cream 5, 8, 12–13
ICEE machine 8
inventors 8, 10, 12, 18, 20

Johnson, Nancy 12

Knedlik, Omar 8
Koops, Matthias 26, 29
Kovats, Tania 24–25

life rafts 20, 23

melting 5–17
molecules 4–5, 25
Munch, Edvard 6

Onishi, Yasuaki 14–15

paper 26–29
printing, 3D 14–15
power, steam 5

Réaumur, René de 29
refrigerators 18–19
rock 4

sculptures 5–6, 14–17, 24
sea salt 25
slushies 8–9
solar stills 20–23
Staite, Prudence 6

Telkes, Maria 20, 23

The Scream 6
turbines 5

Vertical Emptiness FP 14

wasps 29
water 4–5, 7–9, 12–13, 15–17
water vapour 4–5, 23
wax 5, 10–11

DISCOVER MORE...

SCIENCE MAKERS

978 1 5263 0546 6

Making with SOUND

Understanding sound
Found sounds
Talk to the tube
It came from outer space!
AKB48 bottle train
Turn it up!
Underwater ear
Seeing sounds
Get into the groove
Sonic sculpture
Intruder alert!

978 1 5263 0542 8

Making with FORCES

Understanding forces
Speeding car stunt ramp
Newton's cradle
Making flight history
Pressure diver
Rocket power
Floating on air
Whale race
Pendulum art
Kinetic creations
Follow the force!

978 1 5263 0544 2

Making with LIVING THINGS

Understanding living things
Miniature plant world
Fast flowers
Colours of nature
Close-up creepy crawlies
Animal movement
Weave a web
Hear your heart
Body copy
Building blocks of life
Fabulous fossils

978 1 5263 0526 8

Making with LIGHT

Understanding light
Art in shadows
A new view
Curved light
A closer look
Make the world upside-down
Sun prints
Painting with light
Garden gnomon
Lightbox display
Neon sign

978 1 5263 0550 3

Making with MACHINES

How machines work
Thing flinger
Cable delivery!
Powered flight
Weather machine
Bubbles galore!
At the touch of a toe
Snack machine
Flapping bird
Jitter critter
Robot tentacle

978 1 5263 0548 0

Making with STATES OF MATTER

Understanding states of matter
Chocolate art
Summer slushies
Crayon creations
Instant ice cream
Glue gun art
Melting ice people
Desert cooler
Save your life at sea
Evaporation art
Recycled paper

WAYLAND
www.waylandbooks.co.uk